Maria Grazia Calandrone

(°) – seed
and other poems

Translated by Nicholas Benson
Edited with an afterword by Beppe Cavatorta

Opuntia is an imprint of Agincourt Press
Luigi Ballerini and Gianluca Rizzo, Editors
Agincourt Press is a non-profit organization chaired by Berardo Paradiso

All manuscripts are subject to peer review.

All rights reserved.

ISBN: 978-1-946328-42-7

AGINCOURT PRESS
P.O. Box 1039
Cooper Station
New York, NY 10003
www.agincourtbooks.com

© 2024 by Agincourt Press

Contents

from *Fossil Series*   4 / 5

from *The Disappeared*   80 / 81

from *The Moral Good*   88 / 89

Translator's Note   97

Afterword   101

da *Serie Fossile*

from *Fossil Series*

(°) – *seme*

hai una debolezza di spiga,
muscoli di cavalla, un'arsura
di sabbia calpestata
nella spina dorsale
e un solco di aratura,
la solitudine di una bestia santa all'angolo
destro della bocca, dove un'intelligenza
appena nata ti sfiora
quasi senza svegliarti

metti il dito nel solco del tuo cuore, indicami

scopri la crepa tua da dove stilla
il mio sangue sulla foresta dei simboli e nel sonno che specie
di amore
trabocchi
sugli oggetti intorno

      (quanto eccede
la misura del corpo finisce
per agire tra i legamenti elettrici del mondo
come la bruciatura
del neutro – l'inizio
dell'anonimo – poggia con tutto il peso
sulla Terra Straniera del tuo corpo – *per favore
non dirlo, chiudi la bocca*)

(°) – seed

you have the fragility of an ear of wheat,
the muscles of a mare, the heat
of beaten sand
in your spine
and a plowing furrow,
the loneliness of a holy beast in the far
right corner of your mouth, where a newborn
intelligence grazes you
almost without awakening you

put your finger in the furrow of your heart, point to me

you discover your crease where my blood
drops on the forest of symbols, and in sleep may some kind
of love
spill over
onto the objects surrounding

    (whatever exceeds
the limits of the body activates
between the electric ligaments of the world
like the burning
of everything neutral – the beginning
of anonymity – it leans all its weight
on the Foreign Land of your body – *please
don't say it – close your mouth*)

perché il tuo occhio destro sfiora le acque
di un mare sepolto
                       – seme,
profondamente
rovo e corona
di specie
sconosciuta –
         apertamente tace come bronzo, cammina
nel presente
come in un tempio, come nella memoria –
                               fin che dal fondo
dal teatro del mare
una creatura adulta disarmata
si alza in piedi, crede al tuo perdono

23.5.13

because your right eye brushes the water
of a buried sea
                    – deep
bramble and crown,
seed of
an unknown
species –
        silent as bronze out in the open, walk
in the now
as in a temple, as in memory –
                        until from the depths,
from the theater of the sea
an adult creature rises,
unarmed, believing in your mercy

5.23.13

© – *fossile*

metti una mano qui come una benda bianca, chiudimi gli occhi,
colma la soglia di benedizioni, dopo che
sei passata attraverso
l'oro verde dell'iride
come un'ape regale
e – pagliuzza
su pagliuzza,
d'oro e grano trebbiato –
hai fatto di me
il tuo favo di luce

una costellazione di api ruota sul tiglio
con saggezza inumana, un vorticare di intelligenze non si stacca
dall'albero del miele
                      – sarebbe riduttivo dire amore
questa necessità della natura –

                    mentre un vuoto anteriore rimargina
tra fiore e fiore senza lasciare traccia:

                    usa la bocca, sfilami dal cuore
il pungiglione d'oro,
la memoria di un lampo che ha bruciato la mia forma umana
in una qualche preistoria

dove i pazzi accarezzano le pietre come fossero teste di bambini:
                    avvicinati, come la prima

© – *fossil*

put a hand here like a white blindfold, close my eyes,
fill the threshold with blessings, once
you've passed through
the green gold of the iris
like a queen bee
and – straw
upon straw,
of gold and threshed wheat –
you've made me
your honeycomb of light

a constellation of bees swarms on the linden
with inhuman wisdom, a whirlwind of intelligences doesn't leave
the honey tree
     – it would be reductive to call love
this necessity of nature –

     while an anterior void heals
between flower and flower, leaving no trace:

       use your mouth, pull from my heart
the golden stinger,
memory of a flash that seared my human form
in some prehistory

where the mad caress stones like they were children's heads:
    come closer, like the first

tra le cose perdute
e quel volto si leva dalla pietra per sorridere ancora

24.5.13

among lost things
and that face rises from stone to smile again

5.24.13

§ – insufflare

quando l'ape si stacca dal fiore, la sua piccola struttura composta
di righe sature gialle – fatta
da una dottrina di erbe medicamentose – si comporta
come un oggetto di sconosciuta bellezza

quando l'ape si stacca dal fiore, l'intera struttura
dorsale è intaccata da un gelo
lucido e astrale
di bambini lasciati sulla sabbia salata
come costellazioni terrestri
di calce ferma

i bambini abbandonati una volta
se ne vanno per sempre, per sempre
tornano
aspirati dal vento
come campane d'acqua

sono piccole cose che volano,

                                      pula

nella copiosa gratitudine
che consuma quei volti
come cera, perché quelli sono
il neutro, la zona orfana
del mondo – quelli non hanno corpo, hanno grandi e sottili apparati
radicali divelti, ruotano come stelle
sopra il tuo corpo addormentato – entrano

§ – *insufflate*

when the bee lifts from the flower, its minute structure made
of lines saturated with yellow – created
following a doctrine of medicinal herbs – behaves
like an object of unaware beauty

when the bee lifts from the flower, its entire
dorsal structure is damaged by the frost
astral and clear
of children left on saline sand
like terrestrial constellations
of dry lime

children once abandoned
go away forever, forever
return
blown by the wind
like bells of water

they are little things that take flight,

        chaff

in the abundant gratitude
that wears those faces away
like wax, because they are
the neutral, the orphan zone
of the world – they have no body, they have apparatuses, great and subtle
uprooted radicals that rotate like stars
over your sleeping body – they enter

dentro la commozione della tua figura semplicemente
soffiando all'angolo della tua bocca
la bellezza ancora addormentata del mondo, quella
che dal primo giorno
sopportano da soli:

         ora porta con me
lo struggimento, allena tutti i muscoli del corpo
a stare fermi sotto la grande ruota dell'amore:
           solo la perpetua, solo l'insostenibile
bellezza del mondo
verrà travasata
in te come il piú dolce
dei mali, come nell'ancia di una canna che suona – e tu amplificherai
lo splendore del mondo, tu sarai senza involucro
e senza impedimento
maggio muta le rotte dei pianeti
dunque se tocchi il muto della creatura,
il suo piccolo rogo di abbandono
dietro le costole, lei si avvicina come si risaldano i pianeti
all'orbita di Giove
e rinasce

e rinasci
   come dai semi addormentati sotto
la zolla, per un legame impetuoso
di obbedienza primaria, lungo una scala ascendente di
gioia, da tutto il campo appare all'improvviso
l'imperdonabile, la bellezza perduta

25.5.13

the commotion of your figure simply
by puffing into the corner of your mouth
the still-sleeping beauty of the world, which
from the first day
they have borne alone:
                              now carry the grief
with me, train all the muscles of your body
to remain still under the great wheel of love:
                              only the perpetual, only the unsustainable
beauty of the world
will be poured
into you like the sweetest
of ills, as into a sounding reed of cane – and you will amplify
the splendor of the world, you will be without husk
and without hindrance
May changes the planets' orbit
so if you touch the quiet of the creature,
the small wild fire of abandonment
behind her ribcage, she draws close, just as the planets align
in Jupiter's orbit,
and she is reborn

and you are reborn
                    as from seeds asleep under
the turf, in an impetuous link
of primordial obedience, along an ascending staircase of joy,
from all over the field, the unforgivable,
the lost beauty suddenly appears

5.25.13

O – obbedienza

alba: lo senti il rombo dei motori?
                                                se qui
si rifondano i cori
bestiali d'erbe e incantagioni e unguenti
                        è perché ridi come una bambina,
con eccezionale potenza di fuoco
e con perfetta degnità di cuore

fin che lasci colare
          dritto
nel tuorlo a cielo aperto nel mio petto
la prima goccia – densa
come miele – della tua forma

                        algebrica d'amore,
                                  che s'interna
dove il mare rifonda una figura incrollabile,
impasta il sale delle combinazioni
al ritardo del mondo

sei come un balsamo sulla ferita che tu stessa procuri

fino a questa eccedenza ronzante, fino a questa
restituzione
del corpo gigantesco – aumentato
senza circospezione per la via maestra
degli occhi: risale
iniziale

Ο – obedience

alba: do you hear the rumble of engines?
                                                                       if here
the bestial chorus of herbs incantations and unguents
is made anew
                              it's because you laugh like a child,
with the great strength of fire
and the perfect dignity of your heart

as long as you let drip
        directly
into the yolk out in the open into my chest
the first drop – dense
as honey – of your

                            algebraic form of love,
                                                          that withdraws
where the sea makes anew an indestructible figure,
kneads the salt of variations
into the world's belatedness

you are salve on the wound that you yourself cause

up to this buzzing surplus, up to this
restitution
of the giant body – augmented
without caution via the main line
of the eyes: it surfaces
a beginning

dal fondale del tempo, sale dall'acqua pietrificata immobile

è già successo: *davo il nome di amore*
alla gioia che veniva dalla tua bellezza in un campo mai visto
di papaveri e margherite, è già avvenuta questa
comunicazione silenziosa delle radici

oh!, autosufficienza, sterile
antimateria, malignità della ferita aperta

– perfetta
sotto l'ombreggio – bilobata
e sedotta: è già successo
che io mi sollevassi dal bordo del tuo letto come un
        arcobaleno, come una figura di rettitudine, è già
              successo questo poter morire
senza rimpianto – *ti offro la mia vita come qualcosa*
che non ha più valore di un sorriso – questa radice interamente esposta
a causa della dissoluzione della massa terrestre
        – *nel mio sogno parlavi una lingua straniera* –
è già successo che bastasse l'amore come terra

              aerea:

la farfalla sul viso

tutte le ossa come una fascina, una messe completamente scoperta:
        puoi fare del mio cuore
una canna di flauto
per lodare, restituirmi
l'inizio del mondo

27.5.13

from the very backdrop of time, rises from the petrified still water

it happened already: *I gave the name of love*
to the joy that came from your beauty in a never before seen
field of poppies and daisies, it occurred already,
this silent communication of roots

> *o! self-sufficiency, sterile*
> *anti-matter, malignity of the open wound*

– perfect
under the shade – bilobed
and seduced: it already happened
I raised myself from the edge of your bed
        like a rainbow, like a figure of rectitude, it already
                happened, this possibility of dying
without regret – *I offer you my life like something*
not worth more than a smile – this root entirely exposed
because of the dissolution of the terrestrial mass
              – in my dream you were speaking a foreign language –
it already happened that love was enough, like the earth
                          floating:

the butterfly on the face

all the bones in a bundle, a harvest completely exposed:
        you can make of my heart
a flute cane
for sounding praise, to give me back
the beginning of the world

5.27.13

O – radura

profumi di miele barbaro
quando al suono del sistro ti levi
come un incastro di cavallo e femmina, in tutta
                la silenziosa perdizione: una bellezza
semplice e senza sacrificio – spargimento
di melata e di linfa a cielo aperto –
                con le spalle bruciate dal sole, dici
sono immortale
        e d'intorno c'è luce
come acqua abitata da un'entità biologica
rossa e guizzante
                una vena che rapida sul collo
                              è spinta
                                          dal profondo

tamburo del sangue

tutta la terra imita la parola, si adegua alla segreta confidenza degli uomini, piega i cespugli sulla circonferenza del campo affinché essi somiglino a un volto umano

quando il riso si rovescia in pianto e il pianto in uno sguardo
fluido che contiene
in sé ciascuno degli abbandonati

        che perfetto dominio sulle nuvole e che memoria
ha la vita: *ora*
che ti contiene, arriva a certe forze inconfessabili
perché aveva lasciato andare tutto e

O – clearing

scent of wild honey
when you awaken to the sound of the shaker
like horse and woman combined, throughout
                a silent damnation: a beauty
simple and without sacrifice – shedding
of honeydew and lymph, out in the open –
                with sunburned shoulders, you say
I am immortal
        and all around there is light
like water inhabited by a biological entity
red and flickering
        a vein that, rapid on the neck
                      is pushed
                              from the deep

drum of blood

the whole earth imitates the word, adjusts to the secret confidence of man, bends the bushes
on the border of the field, so they resemble a human face

when laughter spills into tears, and tears into a fleeting
look that contains
in itself all the forsaken ones

        what perfect dominion over the clouds and what memory
life has: *now*
that it contains you, it attains particular unsayable strength
because it let everything go, and

il volto
tuo, cosí solo

all'interno, riassume
il genere umano, splende
nel vuoto come un blasone d'oro, come si loda al fuoco della radura
la ferocia del sole, tutto questo rinascere
          ora
      una tecnica bianca di sollevazione
una cosa come vederti sorgere
        – vanificata
e raggiante –
    dalla campagna indemoniata,
    non avere piú nome,

seria come una massa di splendore dire
      sto già cantando, non lo senti?

30.5.13

your face,
so alone

within, embodies
the human type, shines
in the void like a golden coat of arms, as one praises, in the fire of the clearing,
the ferocity of the sun, all this rebirth
          now
       a white technique of rising up
something like watching you lift
         – radiant
and undone –
    from the cursed fields,
    to no longer have a name,

serious as a mass of splendor, saying
       I'm already singing – can't you hear me?

5.30.13

Ω – trono del sole

amore
       – geroglifico
e germoglio –
               accadi:
                       varchi
la soglia, scalzo
e senza volontà – e piú
arrivi inatteso, piú deflagri e trasformi
la memoria in Presente,
portando in te il teatro della lontananza – ed ecco

                                       giugno:
                                       una potenza nera

batte lo zoccolo, tocca zone batteriche dolenti e altri
sentimenti tipici

       (è cosí serio e dolce
       e non ferisce, resta tutta la notte
       curvo sul rossocupo dei tuoi organi, prepara i solchi
       dove seminerà

gioia+gioia, gioia^2 = approvare

lo splendore della costellazione, fermamente
soffiarlo alla superficie del mondo come il silenzio di una cava):
                 che spargimento
sul caldo umano come di lucciole sulla campagna

Ω – throne of the sun

love
       – hieroglyph
and sprout –
               you occur:
                     you cross
the threshold, barefoot
and without will – and the more
you unexpectedly arrive, the more you burst and transform
memory in the Present,
carrying within yourself the theater of distance – and so
                                         it's June:
                                         a dark power

is stamping its hoof, touching infected painful areas, and other
usual feelings

       (it's so serious and sweet
       and doesn't hurt, and stays all night
       bent over the dark red of your organs, prepares the furrows
       where it will sow

joy+joy, joy^2 = to approve

the splendor of the constellation, intently
blowing it over the surface of the world like the silence in a quarry):
               what bloodshed
on human heat, like fireflies on the countryside

notturna, rasa dal vento planetario:
      apri gli occhi – ti dico – *e mancami*, incidi
con l'inchiostro dorato del tuo sguardo il bulbo
dei miei occhi, fanne fiorire
la lingua di fuoco
della ginestra, dopo
che abbiamo abitato
     – soli
come astri – l'effimera
grazia di un mondo fatto per finire
       (sulla riva una canna sfibrata
       dalla lima dell'onda del Nilo)
      con la pietra del cuore
al coperto: cosa?
ha aperto il sipario, che volto
si riaffaccia, impensato e già
indovinato come
indispensabile, dallo scenario aspro delle rocce
e dei rovi

e trascina d'un tratto sulla terra
tutto il vuoto del cielo, tutto il duro

lavoro del cuore, acuto come una febbre primaverile, ascensionale come questa preistoria
ossificata, ormai
cosí vicina da poterla sfiorare
sulle tue labbra, l'origine
del mondo, questa asciutta faccenda
priva di morte, pulita

at night, razed by the planetary wind:
                             open your eyes – I tell you – *and make me miss you*, inscribe
with the golden ink of your gaze the bulb
of my eyes, make them flower
the broom's tongue
of fire, after
we've lived
         – alone
as stars – the ephemeral
grace of a world fated to end
                        (on the shore, a reed bed worn down
                         by the smoothing wave of the Nile)
                     with the stone of the heart
hidden: what
opened the curtain, what face
appears again, unexpected and already
discerned as
indispensable, from the rugged scenery of the rocks
and brambles

and suddenly drags across the earth
all the emptiness of the sky, all the hard

work of the heart, acute as a spring fever, ascensional like this prehistory
ossified now
so close you can brush it
with your lips, the origin
of the world, this dry matter
free of death, clean

come la radice
e come la radice intensamente
fondata,
nel
futuro

1.6.13

as the root
and like the root, intensely
founded
in
the future

6.1.13

H – *seconda vita*

– ape
– cavalla
chiara e ninfale
operaia, lavori nel dolciastro e nel volatile,

                                                                              nel rombo nero

    del polline:

                    una paziente opera socratica cava dal fondo degli
                                   organi muti una radiazione
australe – ti distanzia le ossa (un espandersi come:
                dare – alla – luce) – *pure, quando
ti vedo, scendono le lacrime* a immaginare
la luce calma del tuo viso al mattino
come una terra ben preparata, pronta

                                            sotto
                         un diramarsi di formule stellari
bianche come il sorriso di approvazione
dell'universo alla rossa materia che incastra
carne a carne e volume di terra con l'entità di volo e con la
        stringa densa della voce che altrove, cosí decisa a domare

fa il tuo nome, a sua volta
                        fatto di sciame, approvazione e luce

              – *il verde della vita, lí, attaccata all'acqua*

H – second life

– bee
– mare
lucid nymphal
worker, you work in the sugary and in the volatile,

                                                            in the black rhombus

of pollen:

                patient Socratic work excavating from the base
                              of mute organs an austral
radiation – it creates space between your bones (an expansion like:
                give – to – light) – *and yet, when*
I see you, tears come down imagining
the calm light of your face in the morning
like well-prepared land, ready
                              under
                    a branching of stellar forms
white as the smile of approval
of the universe at the red material that molds
flesh upon flesh and mass of earth to what lifts in flight and
        with the dense thread of the voice that, elsewhere, so set on taming

reveals your name, in turn
                made out of a swarm, approval and light

    – the green of life, there, attached to the water

sbrigliata nella sfida, soffia
dalle narici il fumo della zolla e il fuoco nero della profezia
        – scuote la testa come una radice, ottiene
dal bagliore di latte dell'alba

una soddisfazione cercata e avuta – come avere afferrato un
        pensiero
della materia che fuggiva, una potenza
definitiva – tutta
muscoli e luce, la luce
                laboriosa del mattino sui fiori, l'ombra

nell'incisione dello striato, quella forza
tellurica, primaverile – un'attenzione terrestre
che ha raggiunto una pace primaria, di cielo – *ora*

stai ferma come il cielo, non avere paura
né inquietudine: non hai piú fili d'erba
né seme, *ora*
sei immarcescibile, priva di morte: dimentica

come spingevi l'erba con il muso
come impennavi da cavalcatura, come tenevi il trotto, come ti stancava
questa lotta di forme pseudoumane
contro il peso del cielo
                (la provvisoria ombra di un aereo
sulla fronte abissale della bestia:
                        dall'acciaio
                                della fusoliera

unleashed in the challenge, blowing
earthy smoke from its nostrils and the black fire of prophecy
          – shaking its head like a root, deriving
from the milky bloom of dawn

a sought-after, attained satisfaction – like having plucked
          a thought
from fleeting matter, a definitive
power – all
muscles and light, the light
                              of morning at work on the flowers, the shadow

in the cut of the ridge, that telluric
force, of spring – terrestrial attention
that has attained the peace, original, of the heavens – *now*

stay still as the heavens, have no fear
or dread: you no longer have grass
or seed, *now*
you can spoil no longer, free of death: forget

how you prodded the grass with your muzzle
how you reared up in mid-gallop, as you trotted along, as you grew tired
from this pseudo-human struggle
against the weight of the heavens
                              (the shadow of an airplane passing
on the abyssal forehead of the beast:
                              from the steel
                                        of the fuselage

                              – qualche mano di bianco, una vernice
del colore del sangue – non viene
alcuna opera di silenzio):
                    ti prometto che un giorno

                         il mio sangue sarà
                         la parola che aspetti

                              perdonami, se adesso

chiudo gli occhi per vedere
come vede
il ramo stroncato – se questo
è il numero infinito, se *questo* è il nostro

infinito passato

2.6.13

                              – a coat of white, a varnish

the color of blood – no work
of silence comes):

                              I promise you one day

                                        my blood will be the word
                                        you're waiting for

                                                  forgive me if now

I close my eyes to see
in the way
the severed limb sees – if this
is the infinite number, if *this* is our

infinite past

6.2.13

– rinasce, non ha io

io riconosco la tua bianca soma, la tua bellezza di animale nero, ti slego tutti i filamenti vivi,
                                      finché

sei tutta nuova, splendi nell'erba come una mela
appena fatta – sei la luce dell'alba e sei la mela
e il gesto semplice dell'aratura:
        maschio, femmina, ombra:
              riconosco, qui,
sulle labbra, il punto esatto dell'interruzione – senti

        la nostalgia della preda fuori
dall'umida masticazione della tua bocca, coperta d'oro
        e sali d'altura

e, alla destra, il fulmine, lo scisma, qualcosa come un
              gemito: *sugli occhi*

ho il carico di tutto questo cielo
mosso e grave, di tarda primavera,
      ho il dolore di avere regnato
su un regno abbandonato

    – cosí la scimmia edenica
        si stacca
          – per te –
            scende

– reborn, without an I

I recognize your white flank, your black animal beauty, I loosen all your living filaments
                                                                                                so that

you are entirely new, you shine in the grass like an apple
just created – you are the light of dawn and you are the apple
and the simple act of plowing:
                        male, female, shadow:
                              I recognize, here,
on the lips, the exact point of the interruption – you feel

                      the nostalgia of the prey outside
              the moist chewing of your mouth, covered with gold
                      and salt from the deep

and, to the right, the lightning bolt, the split, something like
                                                a cry: *on the eyes*

I bear the weight of all this sky
rough and grave, of late spring,
                      I have the pain of having reigned
over a forsaken kingdom

       – so the Edenic monkey
                      leaves
                            – for you –
                                    separates

dalla fermezza botanica
del bosco, cresce dall'orizzonte
allo scoperto –
                      aumentata
                      ed esposta, spicca
                                dall'aria i frutti tuttomiele
delle parole,
        tesse il ponte del ricongiungimento, non
finalizzato
a produrre che ricongiungimento:
                            parola

su parola, forgia la lancia del tuo compimento, ti mette a punto come un ingranaggio di cantiere
navale sotto la macina del sole
e i vettori neri delle ali: un risveglio di rondini
sul canale /
                / di taglio, sulle spallette bianche di cemento, fitte
                                            di reti (dentro

guizza argenteo *il pescato*, un raccolto d'uranio e pallore
di sirene platoniche)

l'animale infierisce, non cede,
non si converte, scintilla,
martella, fonde: sta fabbricando, è carsico, desidera
consegnarti – parola per parola – il mondo
tutto spaccato dalla tua eruzione, soggiogato e percosso dal tallone
del semidio, desidera

from the botanic strength
of the forest, grows from the horizon
out in the open –
                reinforced
                and exposed, it plucks
                              from the air the honeyed fruits
of words,
        weaves the bridge of rejoining, not
for any purpose
but to make that rejoining possible:
                              word

after word, he forges the spear of your fulfillment, he fine-tunes you like shipyard
gear under the millstone of the sun
and the black vectors of wings: swallows awakening
over the boat /
                / slip, against shoulders of white concrete, dense
                                            with nets (within

flickers the silvery *catch*, a harvest of uranium and pallor,
of platonic sirens)

the animal rages, does not yield,
does not concede, it glows,
it hammers, melts: it is manufacturing, it is karst, it desires
to deliver you – word upon word – the world
entirely split by your eruption, subdued and shaken by the heel
of the demigod, it desires

posarti nei palmi come una mela
rossa, l'infuocata bellezza
di *questo* mondo
gocciolante dell'amnio del paradiso, non fa che dire:
            prendilo, era tuo

5.6.13

to put in the palm of your hand
like a red apple, the fiery beauty
of *this* world
dripping with heaven's amnion, it keeps saying:
>   *take it, it was always yours*

6.5.13

○ – *all'indimenticabile*

dunque cominci l'opera manuale
sulle disorientate stelle – come
riordinare l'impervia materia
all'inizio del mondo, riallacciare le stelle una all'altra col filo
        di una lacrima – riformare le coppie degli astri: due a due
se ne andavano per il firmamento, compatto
e senza collasso – la materia sapeva
quel che faceva, era
soddisfatta
roteando cosí
lu-mi-no-sa-men-te

                – o –

                        stando ferma cosí, quando doveva,
nella mutezza nera del creato

poi venne il lampo e venne l'atmosfera – e con il lampo venne
        la caduta
della volta celeste:
                      ahi!, rogo
di crematorio, lingua
biforcuta, innalzata fra esangui
monconi
di giuramenti

{il rumore di fondo dello spazio è il rumore domestico delle
stoviglie, che echeggia a lungo
tra le rovine, questo povero modo di tornare umani}

○ – *to the unforgettable*

so begin the manual work
on the bewildered stars – as
setting back in order the impervious matter
at the beginning of the world, reconnecting the stars one to the next by
        the thread of a teardrop – restoring astral couples – two by two
used to go through the firmament, compact
and without collapse – matter knew
what it was doing, it was
satisfied
spinning so
lu-min-ous-ly
                – or –
                        staying still just so, when it needed to,
in the black muteness of creation

then came the flash, and the atmosphere – and with the flash
        came the fall
of the celestial vault:
                o! flame
of the crematorium,
forked tongue, raised among
blood-drained
stumps of oaths

{the noise of the depths of the space is the domestic noise
of pots and pans, this poor way of becoming human again,
echoing at length among the ruins,}

                                                            – a ogni
                                    catastrofe, a ogni bruciatura
del nervo del sollievo (lo tenevi sul petto, il magnete
che ordina il caso e ne fa il tuo destino): per ogni piccolo disastro,
        per un nonnulla in noi

segue il rilascio di un'indifferenza: grigioleggera, lieve come cenere
che non tocca chi tocca
                e non consola – come a levante
                                                brucia
                l'antimateria, lo splendore

nero dell'autosufficienza:

l'antistante, l'astratto
bene di Dio, che sa di diserzione
se non lo strugge
un rimpianto di quanto fu umano

5.6.13

                                          – for every
                              catastrophe, for every burn
at the nerve of relief (you held it to your chest, the magnet
that orders chance and makes it your destiny) – for every little disaster,
        for a trifle in us

the release of an indifference follows: lightgray, light as ash
that leaves untouched whoever touches
                        and does not comfort – as to the east
                                                    antimatter
                                            burns, the black

splendor of self-sufficiency:

the opposing, abstract
good of God, which smells of desertion
if not assailed
by regret for what was human

6.5.13

Θ – per alba

l'anima mia è un dio umano,
                                        un uccello d'altura
che ogni notte nidifica nel chiaro
del tuo petto
come un endecasillabo perfetto
                          (cosa) bianca e copiosa, ala sottile – rosa
                          e roveto, cenere – *parva*
                          tra stelle profuse,
                                   bianco sangue
di spugna tubolare
nel bianco planetario, bianca tigre
seduta ai bordi della bianca strada senza dolore

l'anima mia cresce dalle tue ossa
come una rosa da una lingua viva
        – a stille,
                a emorragia
                        – dal tuo alfabeto
                                  inimmaginabile

ma è da questo corpo,
dalla sua silenziosa mietitura
che viene il verbo,
questo pane assoluto
che ti offro, questa bellezza
viva, fatta per te

6.6.13

Θ – per alba

my soul is a human god,
                           a bird of the heights
that every night nests in the clear
of your chest
like a perfect hendecasyllable
               (thing) white and ample, a slender wing – rose
               and bramble, ash – *parva*
               among profuse stars,
                               white blood
of tubular sponge
in the white planetarium, white tiger
sitting by the side of the white road free from pain

my soul grows from your bones
like a rose from a living tongue
      – in drops,
           in gushes
                – from your unimaginable
                             alphabet

but it is from this body,
from its silent harvest
that the word comes,
this absolute bread
that I offer you, this living
beauty, made for you

6.6.13

α – mal d'aurora

        in che rumore bianco, alla superficie di quale altare,
                in che profanazione

deponi l'incognita del corpo
stretto
dalla neve – corpo
equinoziale

      noumeno – cosa
      pensata –

        – α (alfa) –

            – numero primo – cosa

flessuosa e madida,
genio terrestre,
passo terrestre di volatile
ebbro, cosa
che accade senza volontà,
radice bruna della stella e lupo
sotto il melo

    (se gli vogliamo bene diventa buono *)

un olfatto di cane
ha fiutato

α – aurora sickness

                in what white noise, on the surface of what altar,
                            in what profanation

you deposit the unknown value of the body
constricted
by the snow – equinoctial
body,

        numinous – a thought
        thing –

              – α (alpha) –

                            – prime number – thing

supple and soaked,
earthly genius,
earthly step of a bird
swoon, thing
that happens without will,
brown root of star and wolf
under the apple tree

            (if we love him, he will become docile *)

a dog nose
sniffed out

cosa è rimasto
del corpo perduto
nelle pieghe del mondo, in quale rombo
sotto la terra
ha covato la stessa radice

                                      di quanto

crebbe al sole e finí per mano mia

                    salgo sull'asse cartesiano di un ciliegio carico,
                      tiro giú il sole in un blu d'acqua
                          di vastità irregolare,
                              dal calice blu-notte
                                  delle genziane
                                      levo

un cuore adulto

senza diritto,
                qualcosa
                              che ha deciso
di avere cura,
                sempre,
                          del tuo stupore

14.6.13

what's left
of the lost body
in the folds of the world, in what rumble
under the earth
hatched the same root

                                    and grew

so much in the sun, and ended up in my hand

                I climb the Cartesian axis of a cherry tree laden with fruit,
                      pull down the sun in a blue water
                          of irregular vastness,
                      from the midnight blue chalice
                            of the gentians
                                I lift

an adult heart

without a claim,
            something
                    that decided
to tend
            always
                    to your amazement

6.14.13

✦ – *nihil umbra*

quando pieghi la testa sulla spalla
esponi la parabola radiale
del collo
alla luce del pomeriggio estivo, che rimarca con oro
maturo l'evidenza dei tuoi fianchi

e le tue braccia,
       vivide, nella calce
              spirituale del sole
                      alto sul fosforo dell'erba,
scrivono in aria un verbo mai pensato, un alfabeto fatto per aprirsi
in questa cantica pomeridiana

nuda e semplice, accosti
l'impianto chimico delle mani
ai muscoli del petto, quasi al cuore
                        – e il corpo
                            aperto
cola albume, un segreto
comunicare d'astri,
liquido antrale dolce come un melo

in comune hai il sorriso, l'odore
profondo, di alba
assoluta, miele vergine e latte
che monta
dal corpo vivo

⊚ – *nihil umbra*

when you tilt your head toward your shoulder
you expose the radial parabola
of your neck
to the summer afternoon light, which limns with gold filigree
evidence of your hips

and your arms,
        bright in the spiritual
                lime of the sun,
                        high above the phosphor of the grass,
in the air they write a word never before conceived, an alphabet made to unfurl
in this afternoon canticle

naked and simple, you draw
the chemical force of your hands
to the muscles of the chest, almost to the heart

                                      – and the open
                                              body

drips albumen, a secret
communication of stars,
antral fluid sweet as apple

in common you have the smile, the deep
odor of absolute
dawn, virgin honey and milk
that foams
from the living body

dopo il silenzio della riproduzione

        e gli adduttori fremono
         come erba al vento
e rinasci segreta come il fiore del tiglio dove rinasco, ora che le radici
sotto di noi bevono il caldo della vita nuova

        io che credevo di sapere tutto e non sapevo
         niente di questo amore
sulla soglia, hai la luce
all'altezza del cuore, sposa
alba, fatta d'aria pulita, dici
      con tutto il corpo *ecco, i morti non tornano*

piú, io sono semplice come l'amore, io
sono presente
e limpida: evidente, viva come vita

15.9.13

after the silence of reproduction

       and the adductors tremble
       like grass in a breeze
and you are reborn secret as the flower of the linden where I am reborn, now that the roots
below us drink the warmth of new life

    I who thought I knew everything and didn't know anything
       about this love
on the threshold, you have the light
at heart level, dawn
bride, made of pure air, with your
      whole body you say *behold, no longer do the dead*

return, I am as simple as love, I
am here
and transparent: present and alive as life

9.15.13

® – *mieleambra*

no, l'amore non ha la crudeltà né la dolcezza
dei fenomeni umani: ha la fermezza della vita che sfonda
il suo particolare: si manifesta, prima
      come una sfumatura, d'oro verde e bronzo
      fuso, nelle iridi.
un colore piú denso dello sguardo. l'occhio
non è piú un trasparente occhio umano, è impenetrabile come
oro
– e fisso. noi pensiamo: ripesca dai secoli
lo sguardo della bestia. basica, nel profondo. diciamo: ecco
l'occhio rotondo e senza palpebra
della tigre e dell'aquila. chiamiamo: tigre-amore. mia aquila,
  serpente, asina santa.

ma per quanto ingannarci? quello sguardo è piú intenso
e piú giallo: pensiamo allora
a una zolla di limo, all'immortale
fango dal quale siamo fatti: uno sguardo-deserto. pensiamo
(ah, la bestemmia!
del pensiero): quando eccede il suo limite umano, chi ama
attinge dall'inanimato
il suo colore vasto di deserto e savana.
dunque diciamo: deserto-amore, sguardo immobile della
  natura sola

deserto che rovesci, da quelle orbite disumanate, sopra di me il tuo grano.

® – *honeyamber*

no, love has neither the cruelty nor the sweetness
of human phenomena: it has the firmness of life that breaks through
the particular: it manifests itself, first

                        as a shade, of green gold and molten
                        bronze, in the irises.

a color thicker than a gaze. the eye
is no longer a transparent human eye, it is impenetrable
as gold
– and fixed. we think: from the centuries it retrieves
the gaze of the beast. fundamental, in the depths. we say: here
is the round eye, without an eyelid,
of tiger and eagle. we call it: tiger-love. my eagle.
        serpent. holy donkey.

but how long can we deceive ourselves? that gaze is more intense
and more yellow: so we think
of a lump of silt, of the immortal
clay of which we're made: a desert-gaze. we think
(ah! the blasphemy
of thought!) that when it exceeds human limits, the one who loves
takes on, from the inanimate,
its vast color of desert and savannah.
and so we say: desert-love, motionless gaze
        of solitary nature

desert that, from those uninhabited orbits, pours your grain over me.

non è però spiegata la compattezza, la coerenza rotonda della pietra, viva
al centro dell'essere. né il suo ronzio. diciamo allora: fossile
        (bastava aprirsi
e sentire): cosa comunque
inumana – magnete
prestorico, minerale
neutro
della neutralità della materia.

ma non è tutto: in quello sguardo c'è una pulsazione
involontaria. andiamo indietro, prima dello sguardo
opaco della pietra. andiamo a quando il fossile era vivo. andiamo al gesto:

ecco la goccia d'ambra
che passa sopra l'animale vivo,
la lacrima
dell'albero spaccato, la fibra aperta come un cuore aperto
che trabocca
il caldo della linfa, ecco l'essenza
che si farà pietra, cosa dura
aumentata in bellezza dal suo ospite vivo. imprigionato
        (sembrerebbe) nel traslucente.

ma quello sguardo è il gesto di colare della materia prima
della volontà, che si scinde e rifonde
per contenere altra materia viva: ecco
lo stato liquido del fossile, lo slancio involontario della pietra
quand'era ancora viva e permeabile. quello sguardo è l'assenso della materia

but that doesn't explain the compactness, the circular coherence of stone, alive
in the center of the being. or the buzzing sound. so let's say: fossil
        (it was enough to open up
and feel) yet a thing
not human – prehistoric
magnet, neutral
mineral
from the neutrality of matter.

but that is not all: in that gaze there is an involuntary
pulsation. let's go back, before the opaque
gaze of stone. let's go back to when the fossil was alive. let's go to the gesture:

here is the drop of amber
falling over the living creature,
the teardrop
of the split tree, the fiber open as an open heart
overflowing
the heat of its lymph, here is the essence
that will be made stone, a hard thing
magnified in beauty by its living guest. imprisoned
        (it would seem) in the translucence.

but that gaze is the gesture of the raw matter
of will, splitting and melting down again
to contain other living matter: this
is the liquid state of the fossil, the involuntary momentum of the stone
when it was still alive and permeable. that gaze is the assent of matter

che si schiude e fluisce
verso un'altra creatura della terra
per accoglierla irreparabilmente: un corpoanima
si apre, sgocciola il proprio miele
dentro altri occhi. ogni sua fibra è pronta
a farsi abitare – e, se respinge, ora che fibra
è commista con fibra, deve respingere il suo stesso corpo, deve oscurare il giallo cuore d'ambra.
                                 eccola!

la continua fatica dell'amore: riaprire la materia, il filamento
duro, scostare
   la fibra gialla, fare spazio alla larva dell'amato
nel rogo della pietra, in mezzo al corpo, dipanare la massa
della materia.

                           eccola!

l'incoscienza dell'amore: retrocedere
al gesto primordiale, al *sí*
bello come una scienza naturale: la voce fossile della materia,
da tutte le bocche, da tutte
le fauci, i musi, le cartilagini, dolenti
di gioia e di bellezza degli amanti, continua a dire piú
che io ti amo: continua a dire
sí, come dice il viluppo dell'amore
alla vita che irrimediabilmente
la cambierà. dopo, non c'è ritorno:
     dopo, ogni intercapedine, ogni crepa
lasciata
dai vivi e dai morti alla superficie del mondo
dice: versati!
sul nudo della terra

opening up and flowing
toward another creature of the earth
to accept it irrevocably: a bodysoul
opens, drips its own honey
into other eyes. its every fiber is ready
to be inhabited – and, if it resists, now that fiber
is mixed with fiber, it must repulse its own body, it must cloud the yellow heart of amber.
                                                                                                                   there it is!

the continuous labor of love: to reopen matter, the hard
filament, to push aside
        the yellow fiber, to make room for the larva
of the beloved in the stone pyre, in the center of the body, to unravel the mass
of matter.
                                                                                                     there it is!

the unconsciousness of love: to go back
to the primordial gesture, to the *yes*
beautiful as a natural science: the fossil voice of matter, from
each mouth, from each
jawline, snout, and cartilage, aching
with the joy and beauty of the beloved, continuing to say more
than I love you; it keeps saying
yes, just as the intricacy of love says
yes to the life it will irremediably
change. afterwards, there is no return:
                afterwards, every gap, every wrinkle
left
by the living and the dead on the surface of the world
says: pour yourself out!
onto the naked ground

per raccogliermi,
                gocciola il miele della tua figura sulla mia
figura, assimila a ogni alba
la mia figura in te, rinnova il patto di conservazione. continuamente,
sí, continuamente.

28.9.13

to receive me,
               the honey of your figure drips onto
my figure, each dawn brings
my figure into yours, renews the conservation pact. continually,
yes, continually.

9.28.13

🏛 – *età dell'oro*

dico di quando, per la troppa gioia
d'essere amati, cadiamo
sulla terra *oh!, viva carne*
che perderai la voce
nel pianto, dico di quando
ispirati, noi costruiamo con martello e chiodi lo scenario
e il fossile di un angelo stacca
le ali dalla calce
dei muri, a fondoscena. dico di quando
io abbracciavo in te tutta la vita: la tua
e la mia, che brillavano unite da una gioia preistorica
nella notte, che accadeva da ovest
sulla campagna. dico di quando
tu ritornavi vergine per me
in una trasparente emorragia di luce – oh!, cosa
straordinaria
di natura ordinaria – oh!, vita
tutta intatta, tutta
disordinata, prima che l'amore
pulisca
tutto, all'indietro
tutto, la vita intera

9.10.13

♁ – *the golden age*

I am speaking of when, from the overwhelming
joy at being loved, we fall
to the earth O*! living flesh*
you will lose your voice
in lament I am speaking of when,
inspired, we build the set with hammer and nail,
and the fossil of an angel lifts
its wings from the lime
of the wall, upstage. I am speaking of when
I embraced all of life in you: yours
and mine, glowing and united by a prehistoric joy
in the night, falling over fields
from the west. I am speaking of when
you returned for me, virginal
in a transparent hemorrhage of light—O! wondrous
thing
of ordinary nature—O! life
wholly intact, wholly in
disarray, before love has yet
cleaned up
everything, put back
everything, all of life

10.9.13

l'usignolo

è stato qui un usignolo. non avrebbe dovuto essere qui, ma era qui. e ha cantato tanto. io facevo il mio piccolo canto silenzioso e lui il suo. chissà per chi cantava, forse solo per la dolcezza di cantare. senza scopo, senza vittoria. con la vita all'altezza del suo canto.

è cosí, cara Alba, io cerco che la vita sia all'altezza del canto. è questa la sventura e questo è il bene.

io ti ho tutta vestita del mio canto d'amore
io ti ho tutta innalzata, come erba di marzo che buca
la terra dell'inverno, come il raglio di un'asina tra i cardi
lanaioli, la barra alare gialla
degli uccelli del cielo. la tua vita
ha risposto. il tuo corpo
ha risposto
al mio canto. poi, è tornato nel limite. ma l'usignolo, fuori
tempo e fuori dalla terra
calda d'Africa, qui, dal cuore dell'inverno occidentale

canta, continua, canta

4.1.14

the nightingale

a nightingale was here. it shouldn't have been, but it was. and it sang and sang. I was singing my silent little song, and he was singing his. who knows for whom, maybe just for the pleasure of singing. for no reason, no victory to celebrate. at the height of his song.

and so I search for a life at the height of my song. this, dear Alba, is my misfortune and my blessing.

I have dressed you entirely in my song of love
I have raised you, like the grass in March that pierces
the winter earth, like the braying of a donkey among
wooly thistles, the barred yellow wing
of birds in the sky. your life
responded. your body
responded
to my song. then, it returned to the limit. but the nightingale, out of
sync, and outside the warm
land of Africa, here at the heart of the western winter,

sings and goes on singing

1.4.14

irradia benevolenza

ogni volta che ci veniamo incontro
una creatura inattaccabile
sale dal centro
come una sfera d'oro
e irradia
benevolenza

vedo un ponte che sembra non finire. una struttura bianca,
                         una salita,
             poi l'odore metallico dell'oro – *lasciati*
               respirare – e del corallo fossile
                           sul petto

come le navi entrano nel porto la materia dei vivi riposa.
il gesto viene da una lontananza inaccessibile.

                                     vedo luce nella luce
                                     dei boschi occipitali

e tutto è dolce, anche la stanchezza
nel perdonare. qualcosa di profondo va tenuto immobile.
       uno scarto d'uranio.

                         una bolla di luce, gialla
                 di un giallo minerale, gialla d'oro e di fuoco
                         giallomarino, ci tiene

radiating benevolence

every time we meet each other
an untouchable being
rises from between us
like a golden sphere
and radiates
benevolence

I see a bridge that never seems to end. a white structure,
                                          a rise,
                then the metallic scent of gold – *let yourself*
                    breathe – and of the pink fossil
                                  on the chest

as ships enter port the material of the living rests.
gesture comes from an unreachable distance.

                                                I see light within the light
                                                of the occipital forests

and everything is sweet, even the exhaustion
of forgiving. something profound must be held still.
        a slag of uranium.

                        a bubble of light, mineral
                yellow, the yellow of gold and fire
                    marine-yellow, holds us

come la tigre il giallo della savana,
come l'ambra il suo fossile
e come il corpo tiene il proprio sangue:

             tu corpo radioso
sotto la luce verde del mio sguardo, tu quella che s'illumina e reagisce
dove la volontà non tiene, cosí
iniziale, fertile, confusa
fino nell'intimo della materia.

          e io, lo vedi
cosa sono. una cosa cosí. una cosa umana
che vuole farsi grazia. mischia di gratitudine e materia. cosa umana
che setaccia e raffina
oro dal sangue. ecco l'oro e la scoria
dell'amore umano. lo vedi
cosa sono. una cosa cosí. che però è tua.

6.1.14

as the tiger the yellow of the savannah,
as the amber its fossil
and as the body holds its own blood:

                                                  you, radiant body
under the green light of my gaze, you who light up and respond
where the will can't reach, so
elemental, fertile, confused
right to the innermost matter.

                          and I – you see
what I am. something like this. a human thing
wishing to become grace. a mixture of gratitude and matter. a human thing
that weaves and refines
gold from blood. here is the gold, and the slag
of human love. you see
what I am. something like this. that is yet yours.

1.6.14

sulla ninfea

e continua, continua
come fosse carne, ma è materia di sogni che si china
sul mio corpo,
                fra i capelli
ha un disordine leggero, posa i suoi numeri sulla mia bocca
e i numeri sono la forma della sua bellezza

    sei stata qui con la tua bocca vera, scura
        come una mora di rovo
          e io ero deserto
         che si abbevera
      alle lesioni della carne viva
        e la bacca del cuore
           colava
         miele amaro

oh!, continua, continua
dal punto dello strappo, vieni come scendendo una scala, come se non avessi piú paura

    il mio amore è una membrana che aderisce al suono
        liquido della materia che sei, alla tua voce,
           che è una vibrazione delle corde
             infantili e rimbomba nella
          scatola di costole sternali
        cosí vicina al battito del cuore
      di una madre, al succo pancreatico
      che scioglie zuccheri dietro le fasce addominali,
    mentre sorridi come una piccola benedizione segreta

about the water-lily

and it goes on, goes on
as if it were flesh, but it is dream matter that inclines
over my body,
                       hair
in slight disorder, puts numbers on my mouth
and numbers are the form of its beauty

    you were here with your real mouth, dark
            as a wild blackberry
        and I was a desert
           slaked
      by wounds in the living flesh
      and the berry of the heart
           dripped
           bitter honey

oh! continue—continue
from the instant of the tear, come as though descending stairs, as though no longer afraid

    my love is a membrane that adheres to the liquid
      sound of the matter that you are, to your voice,
          which is a vibration of childhood
              strings and echoes
                in the rib cage
            so close to the heartbeat
        of a mother, to the pancreatic fluid
    dissolving sugars behind the tissue of the abdomen
      while you smile like a little secret blessing

ricomincia da dove
ti sei interrotta, poi
alzati!
come un lembo di vento nelle alte quote, che provoca
un passaggio di nuvole illuminate, alzati come una sorella
vera, portami via
dal grido delle scimmie
che hanno suoni di sabbia
e un'arsura di bestie abbandonate
nella pelliccia, via dal disastro
di addormentarsi
senza aspettare l'alba, senza aspettare piú

20.1.14

start over, from where
you stopped, then
get up!
like a strip of wind up high causing
a procession of bright clouds, rise like a true
sister, take me away
from the parched cries
of the monkeys
and the thirst of beasts forsaken
in their fur, away from the disaster
of falling aslumber
without waiting for sunrise, no longer waiting

1.20.14

Ÿ – *albero, fossile*

verrai nutrita
a lungo, avanti
nel tempo della vita, dai frutti
di un melo preistorico. in un futuro aprile, t'innalzerai
con la spina dorsale spinta
da una linfa nuova,
ricorderai la dolcezza dell'albero che non voleva morire e ributtava e rifioriva, ogni volta
che lo tagliavi. girerai indietro
la testa, allungherai la mano, la bella mano che con tale dolcezza accarezzava
i rami aperti del melo
e mangerai. allora tornerò nella tua bocca con la leggerezza della luce. e ancora,
al calor bianco del nostro tempo estivo, mangerai
la mela che ha pescato
al fondo del tempo, il frutto rosso e gonfio
come un'arteria, che scorre
dalla mia vita alla tua vita,
ma lontano, ma sotto, là dove non arriva la ragione,
nei luoghi inarrestabili. dimentica
l'albero. non pensare piú a niente, soffiami via. che resti solo vita per la tua vita,

24.8.14

Ϋ – tree, fossil

you will be fed
well, all through
your life, with the fruit
of an ancient apple. in a future April, you will rise
with your spine fed
by a new lymph,
you will remember the sweetness of the tree that did not want to die, and revived, and blossomed
[again, every time
you cut it down. you will turn back
your head, you will stretch out your hand, the beautiful hand that with such tenderness caressed
the open branches of the apple tree
and you will eat. then I will return to your mouth with the weightlessness of light. and again,
in the white heat of our summer time, you will eat
the apple found
on the bottom of time, the fruit plump and red
as an artery, flowing
from my life to your life,
but far away, down below, where reason can not reach,
in implacable places. forget
the tree. don't think about anything any longer, puff me away. let only life remain for your life,

8.24.14

da *Gli scomparsi*

from *The Disappeared*

I muschi pavimentano le primavere

Era buio, quella sera – un buio
molto lento e tranquillo – dal quale apparve
la vecchia con lo scialle e la lunga gonna
nera. Disse se vuoi salvare
la tua bambina, lasciala digiuna
tutto il giorno, e la notte le devi
solamente parlare
della grande distanza del paradiso.

Di lei mi resta
il lapsus sulla lingua tra *figlia* e *vita mia*.

Springs are paved by moss

It was dark that evening – a very
still and quiet dark – from which
the old woman appeared, in her shawl
and long black gown. She said: if you want
to save your little girl, have her fast
all day, and at night,
only talk to her
of how far away is paradise.

Of her, I am left
with the lapsus on my tongue, between *daughter* and *life of mine*.

Grafico o golfo della discendenza

In molti la ricordano seduta sui gradini della chiesa – o che dormiva
sparsamente in una macchina abbandonata in riva al fiume
sul quale sono cresciuti i cieli come dischi di luce
investendo i musi delle bestie
basse e mansuete, le lattine traboccanti piogge primaverili.
Sotto la madonna miracolosa alla confluenza dei fiumi
il viso c'era – e il suo orologino, le origini
nascoste nel suo cuore che dorme da settimane sotto il cielo incorrotto
definitivamente limpido.
E più avanti il metallo a ricalco del mare – o una gioia invulnerabile
fin che si estingue l'elemento divino
nell'alta ruota di cenere degli occhi
sporchi e sprecati, labili settimane di vero amore.
Lui si è potuto riconoscere dal lasciapassare
involtato nel cellophane affinché il doppio sogno della identità e
dell'espatrio gli sopravvivesse. Sono
l'uomo che gratta l'angolo del passaporto aspettando il suo turno, sono
quel niente divenuto carne fiammeggiante nelle tue mani.
Nella bocca girano le vaghezze del fondo, l'archeologia lacustre dei loro
occhi di animali
purificati – nudi e montuosi
come la luna che ha spinto lo sguardo sul mare, straripante
re sopravvissuto al diluvio. Queste
le conseguenze del caos e della dimenticanza (interventi
igienici nello spazio
cittadino) e l'amore che spinge a indagare – a essere
feroci: così essi ascoltano

Lineage chart or gulf

Many remember her sitting on the steps of the church – or sleeping
fitfully in an abandoned car on the banks of the river
on which the skies grew like discs of light
glowing on the muzzles of the animals,
lowered mildly, tin cans overflowing with spring rains.
Under the miraculous Madonna at the confluence of the rivers
there was her face – and her little timepiece, the origins
hidden in her heart, asleep for weeks under an uncorrupted,
definitively clear sky.
And further on, the metal tracing the sea – or an invulnerable joy
as long as the divine element is extinguished
in the high wheel of ash of her eyes
dirty and wasted, fleeting weeks of true love.
He could be recognized by the pass
wrapped in cellophane so that the double dream of identity
and expatriation would survive him. I am
the man running his finger along the edge of his passport waiting his turn, I am
that nothingness become flesh aflame in your hands.
In the mouth swirls the indistinct depths, the lake archeology
of their eyes, like those of animals
made pure – naked and mountainous
as the moon that has cast its gaze on the sea, overflowing
king after the deluge. These
are the consequences of chaos and forgetfulness (hygienic interventions
in the space of
the city) and the love that drives us to investigate – to be
ferocious: so they listen

la musica lontana della terra
che ciecamente con le sonde nell'anima e sul greto, li cerca
– gratta via quel coperchio di terra dai loro corpi di agnelli diffidenti.
Ma i bambini ci trovano. Con il cuore bagnato
sotto il piccolo guscio del sole osservano
l'indizio incredulo e costante della nostra bocca e la compresenza
invincibile dei gelsomini appena sopra
le nostre teste – capanne
incustodite di parole odorose di muschio
come i capelli dei fratelli felici
senza indulgenza né circospezione, dai quali viene
una curiosità rovente
una distesa di terra e fermagli, un fronte rasato e ammiccante
di sole diurno – di sole eterno – di eterno.

22 maggio 2004

to the distant music of the earth
that blindly searches for them with probes into the soul and on the banks
– that scrapes the lid of earth off their bodies of distrustful lambs.
But the children find us. With their hearts wet
under the little shell of the sun they observe
the incredulous and constant evidence of our mouths and the invincible
presence of jasmine at the same time
just above our heads – unguarded
huts of words that smell of musk
like the hair of carefree brothers
with neither leniency nor suspicion,
eliciting a burning curiosity,
a field of dirt with hairpins, forehead clear and sparkling
in the sun of day – in the eternal sun – in the eternal.

May 22, 2004

da *Il bene morale*

from *The Moral Good*

da *Le metafore dell'amor perduto*

[...]

3. Ma il mio amore non smette

Non toccarmi, non sono questa cenere
né la salvezza
della carne viva
non la rosa
ma il canto
di una cosa.

Non toccarmi, non sento piú dolore
dell'oggetto composto in tutti i sensi
da superfici: strati
di bianco
fino nel buio della profondità, steli d'aria
dal cuore che è
statue in elevazione
uno stato di cose senza sguardo.

Non toccarmi, non ho piú intelligenza
dell'albero che ciecamente frutta.
Ho sentito qualcosa che sovrastava.
Ho sentito che siamo incorruttibili.
Ecco allora i bambini
monumenti alla gioia
del corpo quando è forte

from *The metaphors of lost love*

[…]

3. But my love doesn't stop

Don't touch me, I am not this ash
nor the salvation
of living flesh
nor the rose
I am but the song
of a thing.

Don't touch me, I no longer feel the pain
of the object composed in every sense
of surfaces: layers
of white
right into the darkness of the depths, stems of air
from the heart
elevated statues
a state of affairs without gaze.

Don't touch me, I have no more intelligence
than the tree that blindly bears fruit.
I felt something overhead.
I heard that we are incorruptible.
So here are the children
monuments to the joy
of the body when it is stronger

piú del dolore, monumenti su coppe di silenzio
e un rumore di botole su lastre bianche.

Non toccarmi, sono la pietra bianca
e l'animale sotto la sua luce senza oggetto
e la parte profonda del cielo come una tunica di rovi
e il ruotare dei rovi.
Sotto il sasso c'è un rivolo di sangue, un insetto
senza speranza
e senza dolore
ma il suo canto si spegnerà per ultimo.

Non toccarmi, ho sognato che in cielo
ruotavano i pianeti e io tra quelli
portavo il cuore
esposto, perché la terra è piccola per il dolore
ma qualcosa perdeva sangue, ancora.

than pain, monuments on bowls of silence
and the sound of trap doors on white slabs.

Don't touch me, I am the white stone
and the animal under its light without object
and the deep part of the sky like a tunic of brambles
and the turning of the brambles.
Under the stone there is a trickle of blood, an insect
without hope
and without pain
but its song will be extinguished last.

Don't touch me, I dreamed that in the sky
the planets were moving, and I was carrying
my exposed heart
among them, because the earth is too small for all the pain,
but something there was still bleeding.

L'idiozia o lo splendore della bellezza

Adesso credo necessario un ottuso atto di fiducia nella bellezza. Agire come non fossimo mai stati. Come non fossimo mai stati traditi. Come se non avessimo visto i nostri cari morire. Agire come se fosse la prima volta. Con la stessa innocenza di Cristo. Con la medesima mortalità elettiva. Abbandoniamo tutta la speranza e tutta la sapienza come il Cristo di Hans Holbein – radice appunto immaginaria de *L'idiota* dostoevskiano – che nemmeno ha interesse a risorgere, che non ha piú interesse a essere divino. Che non ha piú interesse. Ma che, compiuto il dovere di riaprire una strada a suo modo esemplare tra i rovi del mondo, abbandona se stesso – non il suo corpo: se stesso – alla manomissione che una morte completamente umana farà della sua carne. Diventiamo la bellezza perfetta del dio morto, perché solo la fine è infinita e su di essa sola la bellezza si accampa. Assumiamo la bellezza campale del dio morto. Ovvero del perfetto idiota dostoevskiano, che non ha piú la ferita e la nostalgia del risorto di Rilke per l'esperienza regale della finitudine che, nonostante tutto, costruisce imperi di parole. L'idiota agisce come agirà *il Cavaliere* di Hughes. *Egli è il suo stendardo e di quello stracci*. Essere stracci della propria gloria. Essere coscienziosamente carne. Carne mortale. Niente. Dante che sviene continuamente. Mostrare la bellezza di una fine che non scavalca e non trascende se stessa. Carne fatta serena come pietra. Carne completa. L'idiozia della pietra e dell'osso, l'idiozia della cosa, ovvero la piú acuta tra le intelligenze, la piú radicale bellezza e la bontà piú radiante, la bontà idiota che Dostoevskij definiva appunto attraverso la parola *prekrasnyj*, a dire "lo splendore della bellezza".

luglio 2011

The idiocy or the splendor of beauty

Now I think an obtuse act of faith in beauty is necessary. To act as though we've never existed. As though we've never been cheated on. As though we hadn't seen our loved ones die. Act as if it were the first time. With the same innocence of Christ. With the same elective mortality. We abandon all hope and all wisdom like the Christ of Hans Holbein—precisely the imaginary root of Dostoevsky's Idiot—who hasn't the least interest in rising again, who's no longer interested in being divine. Who is no longer interested in anything. But who, having fulfilled the duty of reopening a road in his exemplary way through the brambles of the world, abandons himself—not his body: himself—to the desecration that an entirely human death will wreak on his flesh. We become the perfect beauty of the dead god, because only the end is without end, and on it alone beauty pitches camp. We assume the pastoral beauty of the dead god. That is, of the perfect Dostoevskian idiot, who no longer displays the wound or feels the nostalgia of Rilke's resurrected Christ for the regal sensation of finitude which, in spite of everything, builds empires of words. The idiot acts as the Knight in the poem by Ted Hughes acts. *He is himself his banner and its rags.* To be the rags of one's own glory. To be conscientiously flesh. Mortal flesh. Not more. Dante who keeps on fainting. To display the beauty of an end that neither avoids nor transcends itself. Flesh made serene as stone. Entirely flesh. The idiocy of stone and bone, the idiocy of a thing, or rather the most acute intelligence, most radical beauty, and most radiant goodness, the idiot goodness that Dostoevsky defined precisely with the word *prekrasny*, indicating "the splendor of beauty."

July 2011

Translator's Note

Picking up this book by a contemporary Italian poet, the reader might be expecting something familiar from translations of Ungaretti, Montale, Saba…notice that the Italian poets who come to mind from recent publishing history are male, and that their works are part of a world that has faded away. Certainly more contemporary female poets have been translated of late—Alda Merini, Amelia Rosselli, Antonella Anedda, to name a few—but to less fanfare, and thus far their works are less known.

In any case, no specialized knowledge of context is required for the reader to have an immediate, electric, soul-expanding experience from reading these poems. Calandrone's poetic seems unique in Italian literature, although certainly one may find strands, resonances, elements shared with other poets. But if Calandrone belongs to a gang, it's an international one, in which the corporeal rules the intellectual and the imaginative realm is always informed—yet unbound—by the strictures of the body. Some lines from *insufflate*: "the unsustainable/beauty of the world/will be poured/into you like the sweetest/of ills, as into a sounding reed of

cane—and you will amplify/the splendor of the world,
you will be without husk/and without hindrance [...]"

Sonically and formally, rather than obeying standard forms, Calandrone's lines push out and draw in according to the physical and emotional pressures created by the experience embodied by the poem. In working on this translation, I was always listening to this *respiro*, the music of each poem combining the terrestrial and the interior—and even the *extra*terrestrial, as the reader who goes on to read more of *Fossil Series*, the work from which most of the poems in this volume are taken, will learn.

The reader can expect to feel a measure of dizziness at times, an opening of referentiality on the syntactical level, a kind of vertiginous metaphysical simultaneity: here is an excerpt from the same poem, *insufflate*:

> May changes the planets' orbit
> so if you touch the quiet of the creature,
> the small wild fire of abandonment
> behind her ribcage, she draws close, just as the planets align
> in Jupiter's orbit,
> and she is reborn
> and you are reborn
>   as from seeds asleep under
> the turf, in an impetuous link

> of primordial obedience, along an ascending staircase
> of joy,
> from all over the field, the unforgivable,
> the lost beauty suddenly appears

In discussing this passage with Calandrone, to my question whether the somewhat confusing overlapping of identities was intentional and therefore an appropriate effect of the translation as well, her response was: *Sì, a un certo punto non si capisce più chi è chi!* — Yes, at a certain point one is no longer sure who is who!

Calandrone is an admirer of American poetry, and in a fundamental way her work combines the formal precision of Dickinson with the tactile, open embrace of Whitman. This way of welcoming others is palpable in the poet's curiosity and generosity in the company of other poets, and indeed, the world. I'm very grateful to Maria Grazia Calandrone for her kindness and patience in answering my questions as I worked on these translations. I'm indebted to Beppe Cavatorta, who could well be credited as co-translator, he set me on the right path so often in our discussions of how to render these lines in English. Ultimately this effort is for you, the reader, intended recipient of this book of transformations that, through the alchemy of reading, yet remains new.

Afterword

> *– it would be reductive to call love*
> *this necessity of nature –*
> Maria Grazia Calandrone, *Fossil*

In her *Serie fossile* (*Fossil Series*), acclaimed Italian writer Maria Grazia Calandrone transforms the metaphorical spectrum connected to the idea of "fossil" by turning it –and the process necessary to create it– into the very essence of love. Love is at the core of the entire collection, as the author herself suggests on the back cover: "*Serie fossile* is a poem about love, from the miracle of its birth to the agony of its end." Love, then, is surrender, entailing the complete opening up to the other (*ready to be inhabited*) and irremediable transformation, a rebirth from which there is no going back:

> [...] matter
> opening up and flowing
> toward another creature of the earth
> to accept it irrevocably: a bodysoul
> opens, drips its own honey
> into other eyes. its every fiber is ready
> to be inhabited – and, if it resists, now that fiber
> is mixed with fiber, it must repulse its own body,
>   [it must cloud the yellow heart of amber.
>   there it is!

    the continuous labor of love: to reopen matter, the hard filament, to push aside
        the yellow fiber, to make room for the larva of the beloved in the stone pyre, in the center of the body, [to unravel the mass
of matter.

Shortlisted in 2022 for the prestigious Italian "Premio Strega" with her novel *Splendi come vita* and included among the 5 finalists in the 2023 edition with *Dove non mi hai portata: mia madre, un caso di cronaca*, Maria Grazia Calandrone has become in the last few years one of the most established names in Italian literature. Such recognition is absolutely deserved for an artist who is capable of combining a rediscovered narrative vein in an overturned confessional style with in-depth research work at the core of language, which is apparent in her vast poetic production (her inaugural collection, *Pietra di paragone*, was released in 1998). Additionally and beyond her own craft, Calandrone is a courageous advocate for poetry, which she promotes on programs aired by Rai Radio 3 and through the many collaborative workshops she leads for schools and in programs for the imprisoned.

After her 1998 début, Calandrone published ten poetry collections: *La scimmia randagia* (Crocetti, 2003), *Come per mezzo di una briglia ardente* (Atelier, 2005), *La macchina responsabile* (Crocetti, 2007), *Sulla bocca di tutti* (Crocetti, 2010), *Atto di vita nascente* (Lietocolle 2010), *La vita chiara* (Transeuropa, 2011), *Serie fossile* (Crocetti, 2015), *Gli Scomparsi – storie da "Chi l'ha visto?"* (Lietocolle 2016), *Il bene morale* (Crocetti 2017), and, finally, *Giardino della gioia* (Arnoldo Mondadori Editore 2019). This first American chapbook mainly features poems from *Serie fossile*, with two very brief selections from the two collections that follow it, *Gli scomparsi* and *Il bene morale*.

Released in 2015 for Crocetti and then reprinted in 2020 by Feltrinelli, *Serie fossile* is, in my opinion, the most important work to understand Calandrone's literary trajectory, as it not only marks her full stylistic maturity, but is also a fundamental element to comprehend the reasons behind her two recent novels, both autobiographical and focused respectively, on Consolazione (her adoptive mother) and Lucia, her biological one who took her own life at age 29. Gabriella Maggio, in a rigorous review of Calandrone's last novel, identified a clear connection with *Splendi come vita*: "Love as the light of life, Ariadne's thread in the labyrinth of reality, in its deep gaps. A red thread that stitches together the facts to be collected to form the memory." And love, despite the title of this poetic collection or perhaps because of it, is certainly at the center of *Serie Fossile*.

"Fossilism" is not an uncommon trend in literature, mostly used to highlight the smallness of human life and work compared to the life of Earth itself: it would be impossible not to mention Alessandro Zanella's *Sopra una conchiglia fossile nel mio studio* (Above a fossil shell in my studio) or the comic Venetian passage in Mark Twain's *A Tramp Abroad*, where the narrator, impersonating the classic American tourist who thinks he knows everything when in truth he knows nothing, tries to ridicule the San Marco cathedral and its mosaics by comparing them with the fossil set in the bench on which he sits: "The Cathedral itself had seemed very old; but this picture was illustrating a period in history which made the building seem young by comparison. But I presently found an antique which was older than either the battered Cathedral or the date assigned to the piece of history; it was a spiral-shaped fossil as large as the crown of a hat; it was embedded in the marble bench, and had been sat upon by tourists until it was worn smooth. Contrasted with the inconceivable modest antiquity of this fossil, those other things were flippantly modern--jejune--mere matters of day-before-yesterday."

In line with Zanella's use of fossils, Ralph Waldo Emerson's concept of "language as fossil poetry" and W. H. Auden's thoughts on geology share a profound connection through their exploration of the enduring imprints of the past on the present. Emerson's notion encapsulates the idea that every word we use in language carries within it a rich history, a fossilized fragment of human experience and emotion. In contrast, Auden's musings on geology delve into the geological strata as records of Earth's history, each layer bearing the imprint of ancient events and epochs. Both thoughts illuminate the idea of language and geology as repositories of memory, wherein the past leaves an indelible mark on the present. Emerson's "fossil poetry" metaphor captures the poetic resonance of our words, while Auden's geology offers a tangible, natural parallel to this notion, reminding us that the Earth itself is a vast archive of stories etched in stone. In this convergence, both Emerson and Auden invite us to appreciate the deep, interconnected layers of history and meaning that shape our understanding of the world.

What also emerges from the poems collected in this chapbook is Calandrone's attention to language and its musicality. That is the reason I don't believe it is possible to subscribe to Giorgio Linguaglossa's statement that Calandrone arrives at the "systematic liquidation of the basic metric unit, the hendecasyllable and its replacement with articulated and disjointed phrase units", but rather a wide use of traditional verses –from the hendecasyllable to the septenary– which find new rhythmic and musical functions once they are interposed to prosaic passages or set in between the prolonged and uneven silences of the interspersed spacing.

Calandrone herself seems to suggest that there must be unwavering attention to these forms with an explicit tautological hendecasyllable in *Θ – per alba*: "my soul is a human god, / a bird of the heights / that every night nests in the clear / of your chest / like a perfect hendecasyllable [...]" (l'anima mia è un dio umano, / un uccello d'altura che nidifica nel chiaro /del tuo petto / *come un endecasillabo perfetto* [...]).

Beppe Cavatorta

Tucson, October 15, 2023

About the author

Maria Grazia Calandrone, born in Milan in 1964 and based in Rome, stands as a prominent figure in the realms of poetry, playwriting, journalism, and performance art. Currently serving as the director of cultural programming for RAI Radio 3, she also directs video programs for *Corriere della Sera* web TV and collaborates with Italian TV channels *Rai Letteratura*, *Rai Cultura*, and *Cult Book*, focusing on culture and literature. A passionate advocate for inclusive literature, Calandrone conducts poetry workshops in schools, prisons, and mental health units. Volunteering at the *Piccoli Maestri* children's reading center underscores her commitment to fostering a love for reading among young audiences. Her poetic journey began with the acclaimed *Illustrazioni* (Illustrations, 1994), which received the Eugenio Montale Prize. Calandrone's poetic repertoire includes award-winning works like *Pietra di paragone* (Touchstones, 1998) and *Serie fossile* (Fossil Series, 2015). In addition to her poetic achievements, Calandrone has explored prose with works such as the pseudo-novel *L'infinito mélo* (The Infinite Apple Tree, 2011) the novel *Splendi come vita* (You Shine like Life, 2021), shortlisted for Strega and Campiello Prizes, and *Dove non mi hai portata: Mia madre, un caso di cronaca* (Where You Didn't Take Me. My Mother, A News Story, 2022) her last novel, finalist for the Strega Prize. Calandrone's role as an editor and her involvement in various cultural projects showcase the depth of her impact on the Italian literary landscape. For more information, visit her website at www.mariagraziacalandrone.it.

About the translator

Nicholas Benson holds a PhD in Italian (New York University, 1999) and a MFA in Writing (Vermont College of Fine Arts, 2009). His translations include the following volumes: Attilio Bertolucci's *Winter Journey* (*Viaggio d'inverno*, 2005); Aldo Palazzeschi's *The Arsonist* (*L'incendiario*, 2013), for which he was awarded an NEA Translation Fellowship; and, with Elena Coda, Scipio Slataper's *My Karst and My City* (*Il mio Carso*, 2020), which was awarded the John Florio Prize by the Society of Translators (UK).

About the editor

Beppe Cavatorta is Professor of Italian at the University of Arizona in Tucson. His scholarly articles and translations have been published in numerous journals in the U.S. and Italy. His own poetry has appeared internationally in several journals and in the two chapbooks *La stanza sgombra* (2020) and *Istantanee di un amor de lonh* (2020). He has authored or co-edited ten volumes, among them his monograph, *Viaggio nella narrativa sperimentale italiana del XX secolo* (2013), and the bilingual anthology of Italian Poetry *Those Who from Afar Look Like Flies*, with Luigi Ballerini (tome I, 2017; tome II, forthcoming 2026).

AN OPUNTIA BOOK

Published by Agincourt Press ©2024,
New York, NY, in an edition of
200 copies. Design by
Gary Green. Typeset
in Garamond
Pro.

www.ingramcontent.com/pod-product-compliance
Lightning Source LLC
Chambersburg PA
CBHW030534080526
44586CB00011B/440